KU-213-465

Picture This!

Clothes

Rebecca Rissman

Raintree is an imprint of Capstone Global Library Limited, a company incorporated in England and Wales having its registered office at 7 Pilgrim Street, London, EC4V 6LB – Registered company number: 6695582

To contact Raintree:
Phone: 0845 6044371
Fax: + 44 (0) 1865 312263
Email: myorders@raintreepublishers.co.uk
Outside the UK please telephone +44 1865 312262.

Edited by Daniel Nunn, Catherine Veitch, and Clare Lewis
Designed by Marcus Bell
Picture research by Liz Alexander
Production by Victoria Fitzgerald
Originated by Capstone Global Library Ltd
Printed and bound in China

ISBN 978 1 406 25962 9
17 16 15 14 13
10 9 8 7 6 5 4 3 2 1

British Library Cataloguing in Publication Data
A full catalogue record for this book is available from the British Library.

Acknowledgements
We would like to thank the following for permission to reproduce photographs: Alamy pp. 3 (© Alex Perkins), 4 (© Alex Perkins), 10 (© Corbis Super RF), 18 (© D. Hurst); Getty Images pp. 3 (David Trood/Stone+), 4 (Leon Harris/Cultura), 6 (Grady Reese/the Agency Collection, Digital Vision), 9 (Darrin Klimek/Digital Vision), 16 (Paul Kennedy/Lonely Planet Images), 19 (David Trood/Stone+); iStockphoto p. 5 (© Alan Tobey); Shutterstock pp. 3 (© Bryan Busovicki, © AISPIX by Image Source), 4 (© Yuri Arcurs), 5 (© violetblue, © Sofarina79), 6 (© Yuri Arcurs), 7 (© Katstudio), 8 (© Joyfnp, © Oleg Zabielin, © Bryan Busovicki), 9 (© meunierd, © spirit of America, © Wellford Tiller), 10 (© Monkey Business Images, © spirit of America), 11 (© aarrow, © Stuart Monk, © Mark Herreid, © Andresr), 12 (© BrunoRosa, © testing, © Dmitry Berkut), 13 (© AISPIX by Image Source), 14 (© Fotokostic, © bikeriderlondon, © tankist276, © Tatyana Vychegzhanina), 15 (© iofoto), 16 (© Monkey Business Images, © serrnovik), 17 (© Tracy Whiteside), 18 (© Rdaniel, © Galyna Andrushko, © Styve Reineck), 23 (© Sofarina79); SuperStock p. 5 (Exotica).

Front cover photograph of a group of Geisha, Kyoto, Japan reproduced with permission of Getty Images (Peter Adams/The Image Bank).

Back cover photographs of Irishmen playing bagpipes during the St Patrick's Day Parade reproduced with permission of Shutterstock (© Katstudio).

Every effort has been made to contact copyright holders of material reproduced in this book. Any omissions will be rectified in subsequent printings if notice is given to the publisher.

Contents

Smart clothes

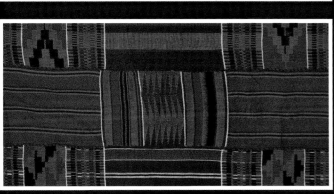

Uniforms

Sports clothes

Outdoor clothes

Find out more about the photos

Page 4 The photos on this page show people dressed for a formal wedding. The woman in the top left photo is wearing a white wedding dress. The man with her is wearing a kilt. The men and boy are wearing smart jackets.

Page 5 The two women shown in the top left and bottom right photos are wearing kimonos in Japan. In the top right photo, a woman is wearing a sari in India. The bottom left photo shows a beautiful piece of kente cloth from Ghana.

Page 6 The photo at the top of this page shows people dressed for a birthday celebration. In the bottom right photo, an actress in Hollywood, California, USA, wears an evening dress. The bottom left photo shows a family dressed for a christening.

Page 7 Irish men in this photo wear kilts in a parade in Montreal, Canada.

Page 8 In the top left photo, a US Marine wears his uniform in front of a Navy ship. In the bottom left photo, a Canadian soldier wears his uniform in the desert. The photo on the right shows a guard wearing a uniform at Buckingham Palace in London.

Page 9 The top left photo shows a member of the Queen's Guard in London. In the top right photo, children in Kenya wear school uniforms. The photo at the bottom left shows a US Marine veteran in his uniform. The bottom right photo shows a police officer wearing her uniform at a police station in the United States.

Page 10 In the top left photo, a nurse in England wears her hospital uniform. The top right photo shows boy scouts wearing uniforms in Los Angeles, California, USA. The photo at the bottom of the page shows girl scouts wearing their uniforms.

Page 11 The photos at the top show marching bands in New York and Minnesota, USA. In the bottom left photo, two pilots wearing their uniforms pose for a photo. In the bottom right photo, a military pilot wears his flight suit.

Page 12 Two photos at the top of this page show swimmers in racing and synchronized swimming suits. At the bottom, two fencers wear protective clothes in a competition in Moscow, Russia.

Page 13 This photo shows a baseball player wearing protective pads and a helmet to keep himself safe.

Page 14 Two photos on this page show footballers wearing their team strip. In the bottom left photo, a gymnast works on the rings in his gymnastics clothing. A rhythmic gymnast wears a leotard in the bottom right photo.

Page 15 An ice hockey player wears warm, padded clothing in this photo.

Page 16 At the top, a surfer in New Zealand wears a rash guard to protect his skin. At the bottom of this page, photos show people wearing warm clothing for cold weather, and a girl wearing a snorkel and mask.

Page 17 Two girls wear raincoats and boots, and carry umbrellas to help them stay dry in the rain.

Page 18 The photo at the top of this page shows a family dressed warmly for ice skating. In the bottom centre photo, a man in Morocco wears a headscarf to protect himself from the sun and stay cool. The two photos at the bottom left and right of the page show people dressed for hiking.

Page 19 A mountain climber wears special shoes to help his feet grip the ice.

Discussion questions

Pages 4–7 show different examples of smart clothes worn around the world.

Can you think of any different types of smart clothes?

When are smart clothes worn?

Why do you think people wear smart clothes?

Do you have any smart clothes? When do you wear them?

Do you wear smart clothes often?

Pages 8–11 show different types of uniforms.

Why do you think people wear uniforms?

What other types of uniforms can you think of?

Have you ever worn a uniform? What was it for? What did it look like?

What kind of uniform does a firefighter wear?

What kind of uniform does a police officer wear?

Which uniforms are brightly coloured? Which uniforms are dull?

Pages 12–15 show people wearing different types of sports clothes.

What makes sports clothing different from other types of clothing?

Why do you think people wear different clothes for sports?

What would happen if the people on these pages wore other types of clothing? For example, what if someone went swimming wearing a coat?

Have you ever worn any sports clothes?

How do some sports clothes help people stay safe?

Why do some sports clothes have the players' names on them?

Pages 16–19 show people in different types of outdoor clothes.

How does the weather affect the types of clothes people wear outdoors?

Do people dress differently for cold weather and hot weather?

What would happen if you wore warm clothes on a hot day?

What if you didn't wear a coat on a very cold day?

How do some outdoor clothes help people stay safe?

What type of outdoor clothes should you wear to go hiking?

What type of outdoor clothes should you wear to go skiing?

All: What is your favourite type of clothing to wear?

Index